TECH IN THE TRENCHES

Strategic Inventions of the French Revolution

Jeri Freedman

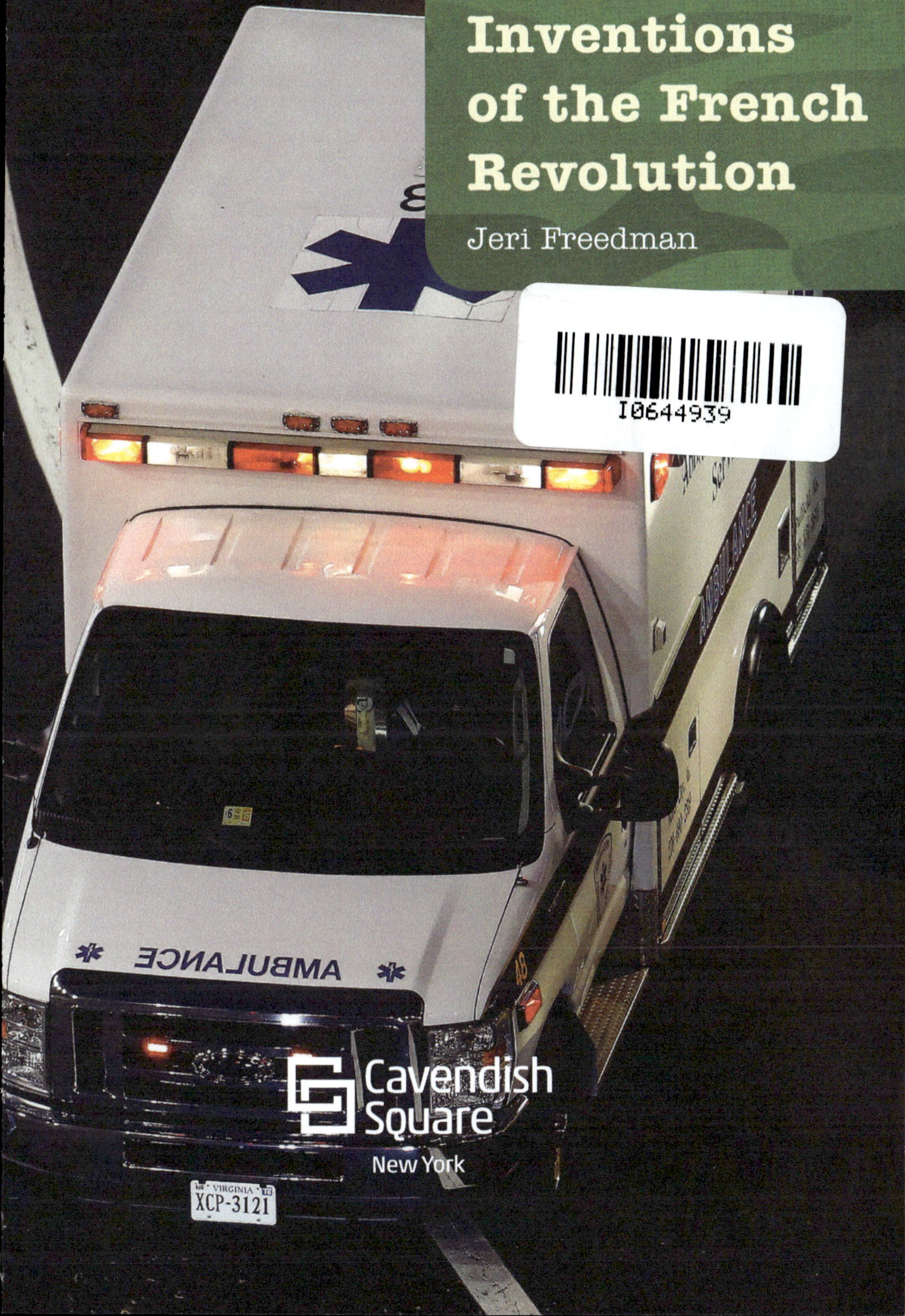

Cavendish Square
New York

Published in 2017 by Cavendish Square Publishing, LLC
243 5th Avenue, Suite 136, New York, NY 10016

First Edition

CPSIA Compliance Information: Batch #CW17CSQ

Library of Congress Cataloging-in-Publication Data

Names: Freedman, Jeri.
Title: Strategic inventions of the French Revolution / Jeri Freedman.
Description: New York : Cavendish Square, 2017. | Series: Tech in the Trenches | Includes index.
Identifiers: ISBN 9781502623478 (library bound) | ISBN 9781502623485 (ebook)
Subjects: LCSH: France--History--Revolution, 1789-1799--Juvenile literature. | Technological innovations--France--History--18th century. | Inventions--France--History--18th century. | Technological innovations--History--Juvenile literature.
Classification: LCC DC148.F74 2017 | DDC 944.04--dc23

Editorial Director: David McNamara
Editor: Kristen Susienka
Copy Editor: Nathan Heidelberger
Associate Art Director: Amy Greenan
Designer: Jessica Nevins
Production Assistant: Karol Szymczuk
Photo Researcher: J8 Media

The photographs in this book are used by permission and through the courtesy of: Cover Tom Pennington/NASCAR/Getty Images; p. 4 Heritage Images/Hulton Archive/Getty Images; pp. 10-11 Horace Vernet/National Gallery/Wikimedia Commons/File: Valmy Battle painting.jpg/Public Domain; pp. 14, 44, 56, 61 Apic/Hulton Archive/Getty Images; p. 22 © North Wind Picture Archives; p. 25 Leemage/Hulton Fine Art Collection/Getty Images; pp. 29, 100 Bettmann/Getty Images; p. 30 Jean-Baptiste Mauzaisse/File:Bataille de Fleurus 1794.JPG/Wikimedia Commons; pp. 36-37 Courtesy of the University of Texas Libraries, The University of Texas at Austin/http://www.lib.utexas.edu/Wikimedia Commons/File: Western Europe 1700.jpg/Public Domain; p. 39 Carle Vernet/http://www.sothebys.com/en/auctions/ecatalogue/2014/old-master-paintings- n09161/lot.92.html/Wikimedia Commons/File: An equestrian portrait of Napoleon with a battle beyond.jpg/Public Domain; p. 46 JLPC/Wikimedia Commons/File: Brouage 17 Canon XVIIe 2014.jpg/Creative Commons Attribution-Share Alike 3.0 Unported; p. 51 Musee de l'Armee, Paris, France/Bridgeman Images; p. 55 Photo 12/Universal Images Group/Getty Images; p. 62 © Mary Evans Picture Library/Alamy Stock Photo; p. 66 Culture Club/Hulton Archive/Getty Images; p. 70 Heritage Images/Hulton Fine Art Collection/Getty Images; p. 76 circle of Jean-Simon Berthelemy/Nagel Auktionen http://www.auction.de/Wikimedia Commons/File:Jean-Simon Berthelemy (circle) Napoleon in the Battle of Maringo.jpg/Public Domain; p. 83 Unknown or not provided/U.S. National Archives and Records Administration/Wikimedia Commons/File: First Ambulance, 1865, US Navy Yard, Mare Island, CA - NARA - 296834.jpg/Public Domain; pp. 86, 93 Print Collector/Hulton Archive/Getty Images; p. 88 Marina Lystseva/TASS/Newscom; p. 98 Museum of the City of New York/Byron Collection/Archive Photos/Getty Images; p. 100 Bettmann/Getty Images.

Printed in the United States of America

CONTENTS

In the Enlightenment, scientists began conducting experiments to understand scientific principles. Here, a scientist named Le Monnier measures the speed at which electricity travels.

INTRODUCTION

An Enlightened Time for Invention

Science and technology permeate every aspect of life today. The roots of much of that science and technology go back to the eighteenth century, often called the Age of Enlightenment. It was an era when science began to replace religion as the guiding principle of life. In the Enlightenment (1600s–1789), everything—including centuries-long methods of government by royalty—was open to question. Philosophers and scientists began to seek scientific solutions to problems, including social problems. Scientists and engineers explored new technologies, such as electricity. New inventions were created. Optical lenses, interchangeable weapon parts, new forms of medical transportation to remove the injured from the battlefield, and the first instances of flight—by hot-air balloon—all changed the industrial and military landscape.

FRANCE'S FOOTPRINTS OF INNOVATION

France in the eighteenth century was a political, cultural, and economic center in Europe. Visitors from around the world came to learn about the latest fashions, art, and science. Spending time in France was part of the Grand Tour that well-off young people took upon completing their education. The French language was the language of culture and commerce throughout the world, much as English is today. Given France's prominence, it was natural that it would be a focal point for new technologies—new ways of thinking.

The science of the eighteenth century built on and continued the inquiries begun by members of the Royal Academy of Sciences, chartered in 1660 by Louis XIV. The academy initially had twenty-one members. The members were supported financially by the French government so that they could devote themselves to the full-time study of science. Likewise, the government covered the cost of printing the results of their scientific investigations. The members met in the Royal Library, dedicating themselves to their research. By the 1700s, there were forty members of the academy, and each member had assistants and associates they were training. At this time, most major cities in France started their own academic societies, which promoted the study of science as well as other subjects. Lectures at these societies were often open to the public and helped popularize the idea that science could improve people's lives. For example, it could provide information to improve agriculture and animal breeding, which would reduce famine and make food more readily available and less expensive. On the eve of the French Revolution, there were fifteen agricultural societies in France seeking to use science to improve the food supply.

RIVALS IN THE WORLD OF INVENTION

Inventions were being developed in every area of life and work at this time throughout the world. British, American, French, German, Italian, and Swiss inventors were all working out the principles and coming up with early models of many of the inventions that became commonplace in the nineteenth, twentieth, and twenty-first centuries. The scientists of the day were largely graduates of European universities. This was not necessarily true of the inventors. However, they were well educated in their own industry and technology, whether that was metallurgy and weapon making or surgery. Prior to the mid-eighteenth century, most skilled craftsmen received their training as apprentices, working for years for a master craftsman to learn their trade.

There was tremendous commercial rivalry between France and Britain during the second half of the eighteenth century. Both nations engaged heavily in trade throughout Europe and around the world. Each encouraged inventors to come up with new and improved products that would outdo the competition.

During the second half of the eighteenth century, the French government established a variety of technical schools throughout the country to train students in industries such as engineering, mining, and military and naval science. This education provided students with an understanding of scientific principles in physics, mathematics, and geology, to name a few. Knowledge of these subjects would allow students to create new technologies and improve old ones. The French government fostered this flowering of technology not only by establishing technical schools but by giving out scholarships to support students on a large scale. The government also granted patents to inventors—a guarantee of the exclusive right to produce (or to license someone else to produce) the invention—for fifteen years. Thus, the government provided a financial incentive for inventors to create new devices. Prior to the mid-1700s, the government had granted exclusive manufacturing rights to favored companies and to guilds. In the mid-1700s, it did away with those privileges.

As the influence of science grew, people began to question the old way of doing things from a societal standpoint as well. Throughout the Middle Ages, the dominant form of government in France—and the rest of Europe—was a monarchy. Kings and queens were believed to rule by "divine right"—that is, they were chosen by God to rule. The lives of the peasants and working-class city dwellers were very hard in the eighteenth century. They were heavily taxed and suffered years of poor harvests. They began to resent the wealth and privileges of the nobility and clergy, and to question the idea of divine right and the differences between those of "higher rank" and themselves.

CHANGES WITH REVOLUTION

Change is disruptive and sometimes chaotic. The French Revolution (1789–1799) reflects these characteristics. The form of the congressional body governing the country changed several times during this period. Throughout, the members of the revolutionary government represented a variety of **factions**, each clinging vigorously to its position. Factions ranged from moderate to liberal to radically left wing. They often fought each other for control of France's future as much as they fought the nobility and clergy.

The period of the revolution, from 1789 to 1799, was a chaotic and often violent time. One faction after another rose to power. Each time a new faction gained control, it endeavored to eliminate those people it thought represented a threat. As time went on, the factions grew angrier and more fearful—and, as a result, more violent. More than seventeen thousand people were executed during the revolution, and thousands more died on the battlefields of Europe.

The wars that occurred during the French Revolution were the result of a clash between two ways of ruling. One way was the traditional monarchy, in which the king and nobility are in control and authority is passed on by birth. The other is the republic, in which people vote for representatives, who then make decisions.

The *Battle of Valmy* by Horace Vernet shows the conflict between the French and Prussian armies on September 20, 1792. The French defeated the Prussians.

During the revolution, the French people rose up and **deposed** the king and the aristocracy. Many of the nobility went into exile in other European countries—but they didn't stay there peacefully. They appealed to other European monarchs to intervene on their behalf and fight to restore the French monarchy. The foreign monarchs themselves feared that if they didn't stop the French revolutionaries from establishing a republic and ruling themselves, their people would start asking the same questions: Why do we need a king and nobility? Why can't we rule ourselves? This would spell the end of their lives of privilege.

At the same time, the revolutionary government of France was doing exactly what the monarchs feared. It was seeking to extend its revolutionary ideas to other countries in Europe and trying to replace those monarchies with a republican government. The result was predictable. War broke out as both sides tried to protect themselves and their ideals.

WAR AND INVENTION

War is a great stimulator of invention, given the ever-present need to find an advantage over the enemy. Modern systems for radio, television, and wireless communication can trace their ancestry back to the optical telegraph system and early experiments in electricity carried out in the late eighteenth century. Emergency medical services, both civilian and military, began with the horse-drawn "flying ambulances" developed by Dominique-Jean Larrey to reduce the death rate among French soldiers during the French Revolutionary Wars. Modern mobile artillery is the descendant of the horse-drawn mobile artillery employed by Napoleon during those wars. Some of Napoleon's tactics are still studied because of their effectiveness.

The most influential inventions of the French Revolution were not technological, however; they were ideas. The Enlightenment ideas that all people have **inherent** rights just by virtue of existing. that the people were capable of ruling themselves, that rulers ruled because people allowed them to, and that people had the right to freedom of choice all fueled political movements that had never been seen before. The twin revolutions in America and France demonstrated that the people could successfully depose monarchs and institute rule by direct representation. In the years following the French Revolution, political change spread around the world as the chains of monarchy were thrown off and new republics arose.

FRENCH INFLUENCE TODAY

The modern era has unfolded in the wake of ideals brought forth by the French Revolution. Both democracy and communism—its rise and fall—have their roots in the ideals of the French Revolution. The rallying cry of the French Revolution, *liberté, égalité, fraternité* (liberty, equality, and fraternity [brotherhood]), became the central **tenet** of political upheavals around the world in the nineteenth, twentieth, and twenty-first centuries as people everywhere fought for the right for freedom and self-rule. These values led to the breakup of European empires in the nineteenth century as colonies fought for independence. Paradoxically, the same values led to the Russian Revolution and the rise of communism in 1916, and to the fall of Russian communism in the 1980s. They influence people's actions every day in modern times, as many people fight for causes such as equal rights and human rights. Nothing has changed the world as much as the ideals that empowered the French Revolution.

Capture of the Bastille. The figure in the foreground symbolizes France; the red, white, and blue colors represent the ideals of liberty, equality, and brotherhood.

CHAPTER ONE

The French Revolution

The French Revolution was a period of violent political and social change in France. It transformed the landscape of the continent by inspiring a wave of revolutions against other monarchies, and it has influenced people's political views all the way to modern times. The revolutionary idea that leaders and governments rule at the will of the ordinary people developed in the context of the Enlightenment, a period in the seventeenth and eighteenth centuries that focused on scientific exploration, resulting in many new inventions and improvements on old technologies.

THE ENLIGHTENMENT

The French Revolution has its roots in the Enlightenment. During this time, philosophers promoted the idea of relying on reason and scientific inquiry rather than on religious or royal doctrine to make decisions and observations about life. Among them were Cesare Beccaria, Voltaire, Denis Diderot, Jean-Jacques Rousseau, David Hume, Adam Smith, and Immanuel Kant. Their works supported the concepts of liberty, technological and social progress, constitutional government rather than monarchy, and the inherent rights of all people, not just those of high birth.

In the 1770s, France played a significant role in the American Revolution (1775–1783), supporting the Americans against the British. Therefore, at the time of the French Revolution, the French people were already aware of the success of the Americans in achieving rule by the people, in line with Enlightenment principles.

THE RISE OF THE PEOPLE

There are many reasons for the French Revolution. One was the economic state of France. The Seven Years' War (1756–1763), in which France played a major role, and France's support of the American Revolution were both expensive. In addition, King Louis XVI's (1754–1793) spending was extravagant, and the royal treasury was **depleted**. Grain harvests had been poor for nearly twenty years, and the price of bread had increased to the point where it was out of reach of the poor. Other agriculture problems, such as the spread of cattle diseases, had led to **deprivation** and widespread unrest among both the peasants and poor city dwellers. There was rising resentment against the privileged clergy and nobility.

Faced with the need to find revenue for the almost bankrupt country, King Louis XVI's comptroller (treasurer), Charles-Alexandre de Calonne, proposed changes in taxation, imposing a property tax on the nobility and clergy, who had previously been exempt from such taxation. To gain support for the tax reform measures and to avoid a revolt by the nobility, Louis XVI convened the Estates-General in 1789. The Estates-General was an assembly of representatives of the clergy, nobility, and the rest of the people. These three groups were known as the "three estates." Representatives of the three estates were to draw up lists of grievances to give to the king. Although the Third Estate was supposedly composed of the general public, in practice it consisted of the male members of the middle class, since those included had to be male citizens at least twenty-five years old who paid taxes.

The members of the Third Estate represented 98 percent of the population, but any measure they voted for could be vetoed by members of the first two estates. Prior to the meeting, the Third Estate attempted to gain support for equal representation and abolition of the veto power of the nobility. They wanted a "one man, one vote" approach. The nobility, as might be expected, did not want to give up their privileges. As animosity grew between the Third Estate and other members of the assembly, the Third Estate broke from the Estates-General on June 17. They formed the National Assembly, which they called an assembly of "people" rather than "estates." The king had locked the assembly doors, so on June 20, they met at an indoor tennis court nearby. They swore an oath (dubbed "The Tennis Court Oath") in which they agreed not to **disperse** until they had achieved constitutional reform. They invited the other estates to join the new assembly, while at the same time making it clear that they would proceed without them. Within a week, most of the clerical deputies and forty-seven liberal nobles out of 291 had joined them. On June 27, the king was forced to acknowledge the new assembly.

STORMING THE BASTILLE

The spark that signaled the start of the French Revolution was the storming of the Bastille, a medieval fortress in Paris that served as the royal prison. It represented the power and authority of the king over the people. The attack took place on July 14, 1789.

That morning, the citizens of France, under the direction of the people's militia—which would later become the revolutionary National Guard—seized the Hôtel des Invalides, an armory housing thousands of muskets. However, the commandant of the facility had removed the 250 barrels of gunpowder to the Bastille for safekeeping. The **partisans** moved to the Bastille, intent on gaining weapons and gunpowder. At 1:30 p.m., the mob filled the outer courtyard. Gunfire erupted. At 3:00 p.m., deserters from the government's French Guards reinforced the partisans, bringing cannons. A large number of royal troops were stationed nearby but refused to intervene. At 5:30, the governor of the prison surrendered, and the mob surged inside.

The storming of the Bastille was symbolic of the triumph of the people's power over the king's. The next morning, the Duke of

La Rochefoucauld told the king about the attack on the Bastille. Louis XVI asked, "Is it a revolt?" "No, Sire," the duke replied, "it's a revolution."

THE DEATH CERTIFICATE OF THE OLD ORDER

Revolutionary fervor spread from Paris throughout the countryside. Resentful of years of oppression, the peasants attacked and burned the homes of nobles, tax collectors, and landlords. This period is known as *la grande peur* (the great fear). As the violence spread, many nobles fled to other countries, where they tried to enlist the aid of foreign monarchs to put down the revolution. They became known as *émigrés*.

On August 4, 1789, the National Assembly signed a document that abolished the special rights of the First and Second Estates. The assembly decreed equality of taxation, legal punishment, and the right to hold office.

THE RIGHTS OF MAN

On August 26, 1789, the National Assembly passed a document entitled the Declaration of the Rights of Man and the Citizen. The Marquis de Lafayette, who had fought against the British in the American Revolution, worked with Thomas Jefferson, author of the Declaration of Independence, and revolutionary leader Honoré Gabriel Riqueti, comte de Mirabeau, to draw up this document. The Declaration of the Rights of Man and the Citizen spelled out the principles that should guide the revolutionary government under the National Assembly.

The declaration stated that all men are born equal and have natural rights to property, liberty, and life. These rights are "natural, **inalienable**, and sacred." The document called for freedom of speech, the press, and religion, and outlawed **arbitrary** arrests. It stated that the government should be elected by the people rather than ruled by the divine right of kings.

Neither the declaration nor other legislation by the assembly established equal rights for all citizens. Only men who paid taxes (which meant property owners) could vote or run for office. Eventually, the right to vote would be extended to all men in the Constitution of Year III in 1795. However, women were still not allowed to vote.

THE WOMEN'S REVOLUTION

Women played an important role in the French Revolution, both individually and collectively. On October 5, 1789, women assembled a list of grievances about issues such as shortages of bread. They assembled in the Parisian markets and marched to the Hôtel de Ville, the seat of city government, demanding that officials address their concerns. When the city officials failed to respond, seven thousand women, armed with cannons and small arms, marched to Versailles, the royal residence. General Lafayette, with twenty thousand troops of National Guardsmen, headed to Versailles to keep order. The women-led mob stormed the palace. Among their demands were that the king and his ministers move from Versailles to Paris, as a sign of good faith, and that they stop trying to block the National Assembly. Lafayette intervened and persuaded the king to agree to relocate the monarchy to Paris.

In 1789, a group of French women presented the Women's Petition to the National Assembly, proposing equal rights for women. When the Constitution of 1791 was passed, disenfranchising women, Olympe de Gouges wrote the Declaration of the Rights of Women. Pointing attention to the contributions of women to the revolution, she called for gender equality. Despite their efforts, women in France did not achieve the right to vote until 1944.

A NEW ORDER

The National Assembly was not a single **homogeneous** group. Within it were different factions, each with its own vision for France. The conservative faction was led by Jacques Antoine Marie de Cazalès, an aristocrat, and Jean-Sifrein Maury, a priest. They were against major changes in the way the country was governed. Because they sat on the right side of the assembly, they became known as "the right wing." A second faction was the *monarchiens*, or Royalist Democrats. They were in favor of a **constitutional monarchy** along the lines of the one in Great Britain. Honoré Mirabeau and Lafayette were prominent members of the moderate National Party. The various factions established revolutionary clubs, where members met to discuss and garner support for their views.

King Louis XVI became more and more fearful of the direction the revolution was taking. Eventually, afraid for his safety, he

A depiction of the "Tennis Court Oath," which formed the first National Assembly.

decided to flee Paris to the Austrian border. The king and his family, including his queen, Marie-Antoinette, had been offered refuge in the camp of French general Bouillé. On the night of June 20, 1791, the royal family disguised themselves as servants and fled from the Tuileries Palace in Paris. Within a day, however, the king was recognized at Varennes in northeastern France. He was arrested and returned to Paris, where he and his family were held under guard.

On September 3, 1791, the National Assembly adopted France's first written constitution. It established a constitutional monarchy, giving the king veto power over laws passed by the assembly, and allowing him to appoint ministers. It represented a compromise between the moderate and leftist factions. However, radicals such as Maximilien de Robespierre (1758–1794), Camille Desmoulins (1760–1794), and Georges Danton (1759–1794) opposed the constitutional monarchy. They began agitating for a republican form of government and the trial of Louis XVI, trying to stir up support among the populace.

DISSENSION WITHIN

The constitution established the Legislative Assembly to replace the National Assembly. The first Legislative Assembly contained members, called deputies, who represented several different factions, including the right-wing Feuillants (constitutional monarchists), the Girondists (liberal republicans), and the radical Jacobins. In the early days of the constitutional monarchy, the king vetoed several pieces of legislation passed by the legislature, including one that threatened the nobles in exile with death. The king's exercising of his veto power angered many people and set the stage for a constitutional crisis.

DEATH OF A KING

As if things weren't bad enough at home, a new threat rose from abroad. Holy Roman Emperor Leopold II; Frederick William II of Prussia; and King Louis XVI's brother, the Comte d'Artois, in exile abroad, issued the Declaration of Pillnitz. The declaration demanded the release of Louis XVI and implied that if he wasn't freed, France would be invaded by Prussia. The French people were infuriated.

In April 1792, believing that the émigrés were forming alliances with the monarchs of Austria and Prussia and planned to attack and attempt to retake the country, the Legislative Assembly declared war on Austria and Prussia. The revolutionaries also hoped to spread their ideas throughout Europe as they took territory there.

At home, the anti-monarchist movement grew in strength. The Commune of Paris was the governing body of the city of Paris, based at the Hôtel de Ville. It consisted of representatives of the forty-eight districts of the city. On August 9, 1792, the existing commune was taken over by a new revolutionary commune, led by Georges Danton, Camille Desmoulins, and Jacques Hébert, which took possession of the Hôtel de Ville. The Legislative Assembly depended on the authority of the commune to remain in power.

This painting by Charles Louis Lucien Müller shows King Louis XVI, Queen Marie-Antoinette, and their children in the royal garden at the Palace of Versailles.

As enemy troops marched toward Paris, the commune began searching for traitors in the city, conducting house-to-house searches. By the end of August, every prison was full. During the night of August 10, 1792, insurgents backed by the militia stormed the Tuileries Palace, killing the Swiss Guards who protected the king and capturing the royal family. The commune imprisoned them in the Temple fortress in Paris. A new legislative body, the National Convention, was hastily called to replace the Legislative Assembly. The convention first met on September 20, 1792. A day later, it abolished the monarchy and declared that France was a republic. The convention consisted of representatives elected by the vote of all French men. It was charged with writing a new constitution and functioned essentially as the government of France. On January 21, 1793, King Louis XVI was condemned to death for high treason and crimes against the state and was executed by guillotine. Nine months later, Marie-Antoinette was executed in the same way.

After the execution of Louis XVI, the country entered a period of war with various European countries. Divisions within the National Convention resulted in extreme turbulence in France.

THE REIGN OF TERROR

On July 13, 1793, Jacobin leader Jean-Paul Marat was assassinated by a member of the Girondin faction, Charlotte Corday. In a power struggle at the National Convention, Maximilien Robespierre succeeded in ousting Georges Danton—the leader of the August 1792 uprising against the king—from the Committee of Public Safety. Robespierre took control of the committee. Under him, the Jacobins initiated the Reign of Terror, a ten-month period from 1793 to 1794, when approximately seventeen thousand people were executed, many without a trial. Most were executed by the guillotine. Finally, in July 1794, fed up with the continuing escalation of the Reign of Terror, a **coalition** of left and right members in the National Convention condemned Robespierre. He was arrested and executed by guillotine on July 28, 1794, marking the end of the Reign of Terror.

THE NEW CONSTITUTION

The National Convention, made up mostly of moderate Girondins who had survived the Reign of Terror, approved a new constitution on August 22, 1795. The new constitution created a legislature with two houses and a five-member Directoire, which acted as the executive branch overseeing the government. The directors would be appointed by parliament.

The Directoire was in charge for four years. Its rule was marked by financial crises and political corruption. By the end of the eighteenth century, only the power of the army was keeping it in power. On November 9, 1799, Napoleon Bonaparte (1769–1821), general of the army, staged a coup d'état. He appointed himself dictator, calling himself France's "first consul," after the rulers of ancient Rome. This event signaled the end of the French Revolution and ushered in the Napoleonic era.

The Guillotine

Perhaps the most famous invention of the French Revolution is the guillotine. Its creation is generally attributed to a French physician named Joseph-Ignace Guillotin. Guillotin was elected to the National Assembly in 1789. However, he did not invent the concept of the guillotine. Guillotine-like devices with an axe blade as the cutting tool were used as far back as the Middle Ages, but Guillotin did design the type of guillotine used during the Reign of Terror. He proposed to the legislature that a law should be passed that required executions to be carried out by means of a machine. In the past, death by beheading was restricted to nobles, because it was seen as a fast and relatively painless death. Common people were executed by hanging, which resulted in slow and painful strangulation, as it was done at the time. Guillotin wanted all those condemned, regardless of class, to be executed in a humane and relatively painless way.

The guillotine was erected on the Place de Grève on April 25, 1792. Soon, the machine became known as the "guillotine" after its designer, a fact that appalled Dr. Guillotin.

The guillotine continued to be the official method of execution for those sentenced to death in France until capital punishment was abolished in 1981. Its last use was in 1977.

Opposite: Charlotte Corday, assassin of prominent revolutionary Jean-Paul Marat, is led to the guillotine. It was used to execute both criminals and those declared to be political enemies of the state.

Fighting in the French Revolutionary Wars was chaotic and bloody. This painting shows a scene from the Battle of Fleurus.

CHAPTER TWO

The French Revolutionary Wars

The French Revolutionary Wars began in 1792 and lasted to around the turn of the nineteenth century. Twice between 1792 and 1802, other countries in Europe formed coalitions against the French, whose revolutionary intent threatened their monarchies, but the bulk of the French Revolutionary Wars took place from 1792 to 1798. This period is called the War of the First Coalition. A second coalition was formed in 1799 and resulted in the War of the Second Coalition (1799–1802), which continued into the early Napoleonic era, when General Napoleon Bonaparte had established himself as dictator of France.

The French Revolutionary Wars started in Europe, but eventually spread as far as the Americas. A decade of warfare left France with control over a large number of territories in Europe and the Louisiana Territory in North America. The French conquests spread revolutionary principles throughout Europe and the Middle East. The wars also resulted in the adoption of professional armies, which employed the latest technology and strategic principles. Many of the approaches used by the French, such as mobile artillery, still influence modern warfare. The global nature of the conflict foreshadowed the world wars of the twentieth century.

PRELUDE TO WAR

King Louis XVI was placed under arrest in 1791, and the monarchy in France was replaced with a republican (elected) government. As a result, France found itself in conflict with other countries in Europe, which had monarchies. Not only did Louis XVI have relatives and allies among the other nations, but the success of the revolution caused other monarchs to fear that such populism might spread to their countries and bring about their downfall.

The Holy Roman emperor and archduke of Austria, Leopold II (1747–1792), was the brother of the queen of France, Marie-Antoinette (1755–1793). Further, the nobles fleeing France and taking refuge in other countries desired for foreign governments to rally in support of Louis XVI. On August 27, 1791, Leopold II met with the king of Prussia, Frederick William II (1744–1797), and together they issued the Declaration of Pillnitz at Pillnitz Castle, near Dresden, Germany. The declaration called on other European monarchs to demand the release of Louis XVI, but it stated that

Austria would only go to war if other European monarchs agreed to do so as well.

Even though Leopold and Friedrich issued the declaration primarily to satisfy the French nobility in exile, the revolutionaries in charge of the French government interpreted it as a threat. They believed that Austria would declare war on France if the king was not freed, which Leopold and Friedrich had no intention of doing. In response, the Legislative Assembly of France declared war on Prussia, Austria, and their allies, in April 1792. Austria and Prussia formed the First Coalition.

THE INVASION OF FRANCE

A Prussian allied army led by Charles William Ferdinand, Duke of Brunswick, assembled at Koblenz on the Rhine in July 1792 and invaded France. It quickly captured the fortresses of Longwy and Verdun. Louis XVI's cousin, Louis Joseph de Bourbon, Prince de Condé, was the leader of an émigré corps within the allied army. He wrote a document that was issued under General Brunswick's signature and became known as the Brunswick Manifesto. It declared that the First Coalition intended to restore the king to power and stated that they would treat all people and towns that opposed them as rebels who were subject to death by martial law. Instead of intimidating the French, the Brunswick Manifesto strengthened their intent to defeat the royalists.

Brunswick began to march toward Paris. On September 20, 1792, he met the French in the Battle of Valmy. French general Charles-François Dumouriez, who had been training his raw troops at Valenciennes, made a daring march past the Prussian advance guard and blocked the road to Paris. He sent word to another general, François-Christophe Kellermann, requesting him to bring troops to assist. Before Kellermann could reach them, the Prussians breached the French line of defense, but when Kellermann arrived, his troops blocked Brunswick, halting his advance.

Key to the success of this and other battles was the French use of artillery. Artillery consists of large guns, such as cannons, on wheels. In earlier wars, artillery was large and heavy and not easily moved. In the French Revolutionary Wars, the French were fighting on many different battlefronts and frequently moving from place to place. They changed the design of cannons and the wheeled base on which they moved so that they were much more mobile. They also made changes in the design of the guns, improving their accuracy. Both infantry (foot soldiers) and cavalry (mounted soldiers) had artillery units that gave the French advantages in battle. At the Battle of Valmy, the artillery performed superbly. The Prussians, having found the campaign more difficult than they had expected, decided it would be too risky and costly to continue, and retreated from France. The next day, the National Convention formally abolished the monarchy and declared France a republic.

THE WAR IN THE NETHERLANDS

General Dumouriez advanced into Belgium. On November 6, 1792, he attacked the Austrians at the Battle of Jemappes. Dumouriez's army was composed mostly of volunteers, whereas the Austrian army, led by Field Marshal Duke Albert of Saxe-Teschen, consisted of professional soldiers. However, the French army outnumbered the Austrians three to one. The French engaged in a series of random attacks on the Austrian position on a strategic ridge, and finally succeeded in seizing part of the area. Despite heavy losses, the Austrians couldn't force them back. Eventually, Saxe-Teschen conceded and withdrew his troops. The success of the French army thrilled the French people and increased the confidence of the government that they could succeed with their military plans.

In January 1793, Great Britain, Spain, and Portugal joined the First Coalition. Dumouriez advanced into the Netherlands. His goal was to take over the country and set up a republic backed by France. Within a month, Dumouriez captured all of the Austrian Netherlands (now Belgium and Holland). However, the Dutch resented the French, and the idea of a republic didn't appeal to many conservative people. Moreover, the coalition armies counterattacked and defeated the French in several battles. In March 1793, Dumouriez attacked a coalition army led by Prince Josias of Saxe-Coburg-Saafield, in the Battle of Neerwinden. The Austrian army along with a small number of Dutch troops beat back the assaults of the French. Dumouriez conceded defeat and was forced to withdraw from Belgium, and Austria regained control of the Austrian Netherlands.

Although he had worked to the best of his ability for the republican government of France, Dumouriez was at heart a royalist. He was appalled by the execution of the king, the general

This map shows the countries of Europe as they were in the 1700s.

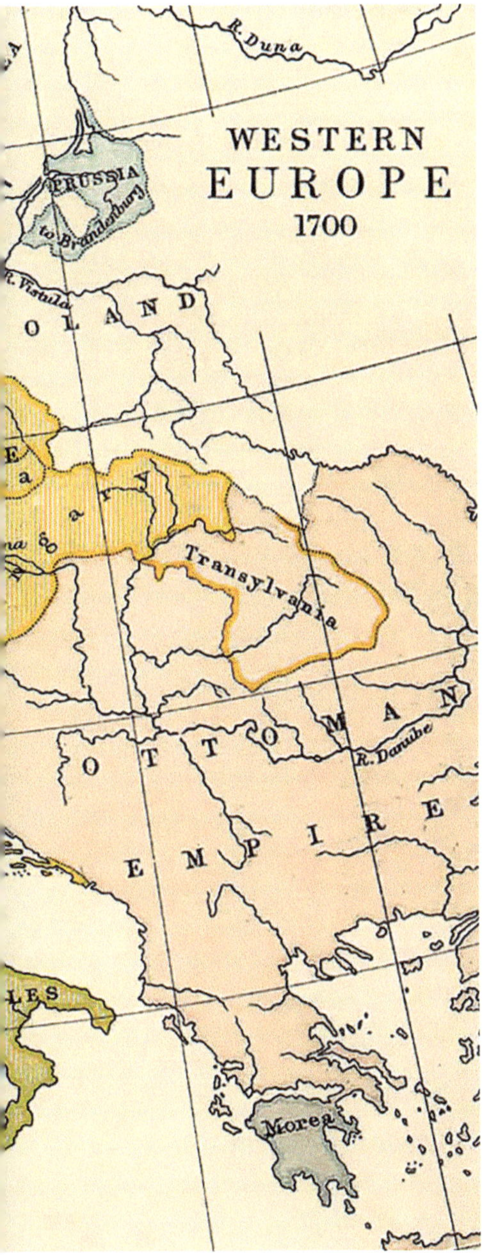

chaos that surrounded the affairs of the new government, and its interference with the way the generals ran the army. He ultimately defected to the Austrians.

A NEW ARMY

The actions of the revolutionary government in Paris did not sit well with many of the more conservative people in the provinces. Revolts occurred in several of them, including Lyon and Marseille. The people of the Vendée went so far as to communicate with the British in a plan to attack the central government in Paris. Meanwhile, Sardinian armies crossed the Alps, and Spanish armies crossed the Pyrenees Mountains, approaching France. Austrian armies drove the northern French armies out of Valenciennes and

Napoleon

Napoleon Bonaparte rose to prominence during the French Revolution. A young lieutenant at the beginning of the French Revolutionary Wars, he became general over the entire army by their end, and ultimately the first emperor of France. Under his control, the army implemented many advances in weaponry, communications, and the medical treatment of soldiers.

Napoleon was born on the island of Corsica to a moderately well-off family descended from the Italian aristocracy. In May 1779, he was accepted at a military academy in Brienne-le-Château. He read widely, particularly history and geography, and excelled at mathematics. When he graduated in 1784, he trained to become an artillery officer at the prestigious École Militaire (Military School) in Paris. His knowledge of artillery and mathematics provided him the knowledge to revolutionize the way artillery was used in war.

Napoleon served in the French army beginning in 1789. From the start of the French Revolution, Napoleon supported revolutionary ideas. He tried to spread these ideals to his native Corsica but failed, and he was banished from the island in 1793. In 1795, when the governing Directoire of France was under attack by royalists, Napoleon saved it by attacking the insurgents with artillery. The Directoire rewarded Napoleon by giving him command of the French Army of Italy, even though he was only twenty-six years old. It was his first campaign, but his decisive victories against the Austrians and their Italian allies made him famous. He not only was instrumental in France's success in the revolutionary wars but would go on to a further series of conquests in the Napoleonic Wars in the early nineteenth century.

Napoleon directs troops in battle. Napoleon began his military career during the French Revolutionary Wars and ultimately conquered much of western Europe.

occupied the area. Then, on May 31, 1793, Great Britain prepared for a naval blockade of France.

In response, the revolutionary government called for a full-scale draft, creating a force of 750,00 to 800,000 soldiers, distributed across fourteen armies. By the end of the year, the French were gaining ground. In September, Nicolas Houchard forced the Duke of York to abandon the siege of Dunkirk. In October, the northern armies won the Battle of Wattignies against the Austrians. Winter put an end to further advances.

THE FLANDERS CAMPAIGN AND RECOGNIZING FRANCE

In 1794, in the Flanders campaign, the French and Austrians attacked each other. The Austrians besieged the town of Landrecies and advanced towards Mons and Maubeuge. The French launched offensives on multiple fronts, with two armies attacking from Flanders and one attacking from the German border. The French fought several battles that ended in a stalemate before winning at the battles of Tourcoing and Fleurus in June. Ultimately, the French armies drove the Austrians, British, and Dutch beyond the Rhine. The French occupied Belgium, the southern Netherlands, and the Rhineland. The French navy was also victorious in 1794, holding off a British attempt to block a vital shipment of grain from America.

By 1795, many people in Holland were fed up with William V, the ruler of the country. They attempted to overthrow the government as the French had done but were unsuccessful.

The Manufacture of Paris

The French Revolutionary Wars were not just wars of soldiers, but also wars of engineers. Armies need weapons, and in revolutionary France there were not enough. In April 1794, the revolutionary government of France undertook a massive industrial production project called the Manufacture of Paris. It was designed to make Paris the European center of musket production. In charge of the project were two military engineers: Lazare Carnot and Claude-Antoine Prieur, often called Prieur de la Côte-d'Or. The two men were dubbed "Organizers of Victory." They established a secret site for testing new weapons and created an organization of tech-savvy technicians, armorers, and metalworkers. The military engineers controlled the weapons the armies used in the field and oversaw the production of weapons. When the revolutionary government ordered universal **conscription** for men between the ages of eighteen and twenty-five, it also decreed that the rest of the population "constituted an army occupied with the production of arms."

At the height of production, the Manufacture employed more than five thousand people in thirty government workshops. Because workers couldn't become skilled in areas such as metalwork quickly enough, the government created the "Workshop of Perfectibility," where experiments were carried out to create machine tools that could make interchangeable parts for firearms. These could be used by semiskilled labor to assemble weapons at high speed, without the need for each weapon to be created by skilled craftsman. This approach, influenced by the scientific ideas of the Enlightenment, reflected a new attitude to the creation of goods that would affect manufacturing for centuries afterward.

When the French forces invaded the Netherlands, they were welcomed by these rebels, who joined the cause rather than fighting the French. City after city fell to the French. The French captured the Dutch fleet, and William V fled to Britain. The Batavian Republic was formed in the Netherlands, and it retained close ties to the French Republic. In the wake of the loss of the Netherlands, the Prussians abandoned the coalition, and on April 6, 1795, they signed the Peace of Basel with the French.

In Spain, the French army was also victorious. They captured Bilbao and Vitoria as they advanced through Catalonia, heading toward Castile. In the face of the French advance, Spain also decided to make a peace agreement with the French, officially recognizing the revolutionary government.

THE WAR IN ITALY

In 1795, in northern Italy, the French army was in a strong position to attack the Austrian and Sardinian forces, but the general of the army there was reluctant to move. He was replaced by Napoleon Bonaparte.

In 1796, Napoleon embarked on a bold invasion of Italy. The army marched over the Apennines near Altare to attack the enemy position at Ceva. The Austrian troops, led by Johann Beaullieu, attacked the eastern side of the French forces near Genoa. This left the right wing of the coalition forces isolated, and Napoleon attacked and crushed them. The following day, he beat the Austrian and Sardinian forces at Milesimo. Then, at Dego, he drove the Austrians northeast, which separated them from their

Piedmontese allies. The French next trounced the Piedmontese in the Battle of Mondovì. The Piedmontese signed a peace treaty with the French and ceded Savoy and Nice. Control of those cities provided the French with bases from which to attack the Austrians in the Netherlands. Napoleon's forces crossed the Po River and cut off the Austrians' line of retreat. The French and Austrians continued to battle each other in Italy throughout the rest of the year. Ultimately, the French prevailed and drove the Austrians back to the Tyrol.

The French set their sights on Austria. Napoleon defeated Archduke Charles of Austria at Tagliamento in March 1797, then went on to the Austrian capital, Vienna. In Germany, two French armies, led by Generals Hoche and Moreau, advanced across the Rhine. The French victories intimidated the Austrians. They sued for peace and signed a peace treaty in April 1797. The French gained the Austrian Netherlands, and the Austrians agreed that the French border would extend to the Rhine River.

WAR IN THE MIDDLE EAST

Napoleon's next campaign was not as successful as his previous ones. In 1798, Napoleon came up with a plan to conquer Egypt and Syria. One goal was to establish a French presence in the Middle East and disrupt Britain's trade with India, since the French were still at war with Britain. The Directoire, the revolutionary collective ruling France, thought that Napoleon was getting too powerful, and therefore supported the idea, since the campaign would remove him from France. Napoleon sailed a naval

During Napoleon's Egyptian campaign, troops fought in the desert as they attempted to reach the city of Cairo. The soldiers had to survive harsh conditions as well as the enemy.

force to Egypt, as well as bringing a large land force. He captured the island of Malta en route to Egypt, and he won the Battle of the Pyramids at Giza, near Cairo. In this battle, he made the most of his mobile artillery. He used a large square composed of infantry soldiers with artillery in the center, hammering the enemy with artillery they couldn't reach. The French forces then took Cairo.

At that point, the British naval fleet, under the command of Admiral Horatio Nelson, located the French fleet and defeated it in the Battle of the Nile. Much of Napoleon's fleet was destroyed, but his army remained in control of Egypt until 1801. In 1799, Napoleon attempted to capture the city of Acre in Syria but failed. After making sure Egypt was secure, he returned to France.

In 1799, various countries came together to create the Second Coalition. It included Britain, Russia, the Ottoman Empire, Naples, Portugal, Austria, and Germany. They attempted to invade the Netherlands but were defeated by the French. They were more successful in Italy and Switzerland, driving back the French armies there. In November 1799, Napoleon staged a coup and took control of the French government, establishing himself as "First Consul of France," and changing France from a republic to a dictatorship.

Artillery like this cannon was packed with gunpowder and a projectile. The gunpowder was ignited by a lit fuse and propelled the projectile across a large distance.

CHAPTER THREE

Mobile Artillery

Prior to the French Revolutionary Wars, battles were primarily conducted with groups of infantry (foot soldiers) armed with muskets and groups of cavalry (mounted horseman). Artillery was primarily used for knocking down walls of fortresses in sieges and as backup for infantry. Advances in artillery in the late 1700s made it a more important and versatile weapon.

ARTILLERY

The term "artillery" refers to large pieces of military equipment capable of propelling a projectile far beyond the range of a handheld gun. The cannon was the most common type of artillery used up to the time of the French Revolution. A cannon uses explosive propellants to launch a projectile, and the most commonly used propellant of the time was gunpowder. Cannons vary in size and shape, which affect their mobility, rate of fire, and force. The word "cannon" means "tube," which refers to the tube-like barrel from which a projectile is launched. The cannon consists of the barrel and a base or cradle onto which the barrel is mounted. The gunpowder and projectile are loaded into the cannon, and the gunpowder is ignited. It explodes, propelling the projectile forward.

Field artillery cannons in Europe were primarily made of bronze, although some later models were made of cast iron. Bronze was heavy and expensive, but it was superior to iron in flexibility, which made it less likely to explode from the high pressure when the charge was set off. In contrast, cast-iron cannons were less expensive and lasted longer in the field because they could be fired more times without deteriorating. Cast-iron cannons had a tendency to burst without any warning signs of wear, which made them more dangerous to use. The most common—and stable—form of cannon was front loaded. Gunpowder was scooped into the tube with a tool called a ladle; then the shot was loaded. After the load was tamped down with another long-handled tool, a torch was used to light the gunpowder through a torch hole at the end of the tube. Later cannons were sometimes breech loaded, which meant the charge was inserted into the breech, or side, of the gun.

THE HISTORY OF ARTILLERY

Cannons were invented in China in the twelfth century and are one of the earliest types of gunpowder-based artillery. Spain and Portugal were the first countries to use cannons in Europe, in the thirteenth century. Cannons were commonly used in siege and anti-infantry actions during the later Middle Ages.

Fixed artillery pieces were used for sieges in medieval warfare. Bombards were large cannons without a carriage that were fixed in place and used to shoot projectiles that would knock down the walls of fortresses being besieged.

A field cannon, in contrast, was mounted on a carriage with wheels and an axle. Pulled by animals, this weapon could be moved with the army instead of being fixed in place. However, cannons of the seventeenth century were still very large and cumbersome to move. Infantry with muskets, not artillery, were the mainstay of military conflict.

ARTILLERY IN THE 1600S AND 1700s

In the seventeenth century, new forms of artillery were developed, including howitzers and mortars, and shells, rather than cannonballs or other solid shot, were used. Shells are hollow and filled with explosive material or **shrapnel**. Howitzers are heavy guns fired at high velocity and long range. Mortars are lighter, low-velocity weapons that are fired at short ranges.

Antoine-Laurent Lavoisier

In order to fire a projectile from a cannon, gunpowder was ignited, using oxygen to burn. The resulting explosion propelled the projectile from the gun. Better quality gunpowder results in a more powerful force. Antoine-Laurent Lavoisier was a French scientist who studied the reactions of other elements with oxygen. His work revealed important information about **combustion** that led to better performance by artillery weapons. He was the son of a wealthy Parisian lawyer and obtained a law degree, but while in college he also studied the sciences, which were his true interest. His earliest scientific work was in geology, and as a result of his contributions to the field, he was elected to the prestigious Academy of Sciences in 1769, at the age of twenty-five. That year he also bought a share in a commercial company that collected taxes for the crown.

In 1775, Lavoisier was appointed a commissioner of the Royal Gunpowder and Saltpeter Administration, a position that allowed him to set up a well-equipped laboratory at the Paris arsenal. Among his discoveries, Lavoisier established the role of oxygen in combustion. He contributed to French military efforts by developing a method to produce more and better gunpowder by improving the purity of the constituents—saltpeter (potassium nitrate), sulfur, and charcoal. He also developed a better method of granulating the powder for better combustion. Better gunpowder meant more efficient and accurate weapons.

Lavoisier was an avid supporter of the French Revolution. He wrote reports advocating reforms, including the development of the metric system to ensure an accurate system of weights and measures. However, he made an enemy of the revolutionary leader Jean-Paul Marat, who denounced him during the Reign of Terror as an enemy of the revolution because he was a former collector of taxes. As a result, he was guillotined in 1794.

French mobile artillery could be easily moved on wheeled carriages.

In the 1700s, for the first time, artillery became an integral part of military campaigns rather than simply a backup for infantry or a means of besieging walled fortifications. In the 1740s, a Prussian artilleryman named Ernst von Holtzman invented the screw quoin, a device for accurately raising and lowering the barrel of an artillery gun. It was basically a wooden wedge placed under the barrel and adjusted by means of a screw to change the elevation of the barrel, which was critical to accurate firing. Lieutenant-General Brocard invented the first artillery cartridge, combining shot and gunpowder, in the 1740s. Bernard Forest de Beldor (1698–1761) was a mathematician working as an instructor at the French artillery schools. He proved that a much smaller load of powder could fire a projectile with the same force and distance as the large quantities previously used. His calculations meant that artillery tubes could be made much lighter because the thickness required to withstand the force of the charge was reduced. These weapons were easier to move and required fewer horses to pull.

The major breakthrough came during the Seven Years' War, which preceded the French Revolution. King Frederick II of Prussia (1740–1786) reorganized his armies. One of his improvements was the formation of the first complete units of horse artillery. Large numbers of mobile artillery were pulled by teams of horses and could be quickly moved around the battlefield. This approach was adopted by Napoleon in his battles.

At this time, a flintlock firing mechanism was developed by the French to replace the slower matchlock method of lighting the powder through a torch hole. In a flintlock mechanism, a lock is released and hits a piece of flint, creating a spark, which ignites the gunpowder in a gun. In the old method, an open flame had to be held to the torch hole to set off the gunpowder. The new method was not only more efficient but safer.

THE GRIBEAUVAL SYSTEM

Jean-Baptiste de Gribeauval (1715–1789) was a French artillery engineer. He developed the most complete and advanced artillery system of the eighteenth century. Gribeauval joined the army in 1732 and became an artillery officer in 1735. From the beginning, he displayed a knack for improving artillery. In 1748, he designed a new type of carriage for fortress guns. In 1752, he took a trip to Prussia to study their artillery, which was the most advanced light artillery of the time. He brought copies of the Prussian designs back to France and built and tested artillery based on them. From 1757 to 1762, he was stationed in Austria, where he took the opportunity to study and copy Austrian light artillery pieces.

When he returned to France in 1762, he wrote the French minister of war, stating that he wanted to develop a new system of light artillery to replace the old-fashioned system currently in use. He modernized the gun carriages and tube, creating a design more advanced than the Austrian or Prussian artillery. His designs made the guns simpler to use, more mobile, and more accurate. When a gun fires a projectile forward, the force of the exploding cartridge shoves the rear of the gun backward. This is known as recoil, and it affects the accuracy of the gun. One of Gribeauval's innovations was to incorporate a curve into the carriage of the gun so that it would absorb much of the backward and downward recoil. Some of his other innovations included using an axle and brass wheel hubs, which made the guns easier to move. He also added a fixed front sight for aiming, an adjustable rear sight that didn't have to be removed for firing, and a new type of elevating screw to raise and lower the gun's tube.

In the mid-eighteenth century, Gribeauval standardized the production of cannons. Using standard designs for the various parts of the cannon made it possible to quickly repair cannons in the field. His innovations also sped up cannon production.

Prior to Gribeauval's innovations, every part of every gun was handmade by craftsmen. Because their measurements varied slightly, parts that needed to be replaced had to be custom made. Everything about Gribeauval's system was designed to create *mobile* artillery. Artillery guns are named according to the size of the load they shoot. With Gribeauval's redesigned artillery, 4-pound (1.8-kilogram) and 8-pound (3.6 kg) guns could be pulled by four horses, and 12-pounders (5.4 kg) by six horses. Previously, as many as twelve horses would have been required to move an artillery piece. Gribeauval was made inspector general of artillery in 1776. His system was used in the Revolutionary and Napoleonic Wars and was one of the main reasons for the French army's success.

Napoleon was an ex–artillery officer. His familiarity with the technology allowed him to see the ways in which batteries of artillery pieces could be used to advantage. He established both infantry and cavalry artillery units. Infantry gunners walked behind their artillery pieces, which were pulled by draft horses. Cavalry gunners either rode a horse or traveled on horse-drawn vehicles. There was also mountain artillery, which could be disassembled, packed on mules, and then reassembled on site.

Artillery weapons are most effective when massed in large numbers. The improvements that resulted in smaller, more powerful weapons made it possible to move them with both cavalry and infantry troops, and to use them en masse for a devastating barrage of firepower. This new approach to warfare was one of the reasons for the many successes of the French Revolutionary army.

Jean-Baptiste de Gribeauval

This illustration shows Claude Chappe. His optical telegraph was the world's first telecommunications system.

CHAPTER FOUR

The Optical Telegraph

During the French Revolution, Claude Chappe (1763–1805) invented the first countrywide communications system—an optical telegraph system. It took minutes to transmit messages by means of Chappe's system, while sending a message by messenger took days. The ability to transmit messages quickly provided a major benefit to the French government and military. Eventually expanded to 556 towers, the system crossed France and extended into a number of other European cities, including Amsterdam, Brussels, Milan, and Venice. In total, the system covered 3,000 miles (4,800 kilometers).

WHAT IS TELEGRAPHY?

"Telegraphy" comes from the Greek words *tele,* meaning "at a distance," and *graphein,* meaning "writing." Thus, "telegraphy" means "writing at a distance." It refers to the transmission of messages from one point to a distant location, by any method.

Telegraphic communication can take many forms—from smoke signals to colored flags to electrical pulses. Prior to the invention of Chappe's optical telegraph system, communication systems relied on messengers, pigeons, or **semaphore** using flags, fire beacons, and the like. The roots of the optical telegraph systems lie in semaphore, which sends signals by means of objects that can be viewed at a distance, such as flags, smoke, or reflected light. Scientists experimented with electrical telegraphy as early as the eighteenth century. However, issues such as the lack of adequate insulation for wires made it impossible to develop a reliable system. Therefore, in the mid to late eighteenth century, a method relying on optical signals remained the best option for a successful telegraphic system.

OPTICAL TELEGRAPHY

Claude Chappe was a French priest born in 1763 in Brûlon, France. Claude and his three brothers were given college educations by their affluent father. When Claude completed his education at the seminary and entered the priesthood, he was given a well-paying post in Paris. Even then, he spent much of his time conducting experiments in physics.

When the French Revolution occurred, with its **anticlerical** attacks, he lost his position and returned to the family home in Brûlon, where he continued his experiments. The central government of revolutionary France needed a speedy, dependable communications system to conduct its war efforts against Britain, the Netherlands, Austria, Prussia, and Spain. Claude's brother Ignace was in the Legislative Assembly, so Claude was aware of this problem. With the assistance of his three brothers, in the early 1790s he invented a system of telegraphy that could be used to transmit complicated messages over long distances at any time, day or night.

In 1790, the Chappe brothers began to devise a means of communication that would allow the government to send orders and receive military intelligence quickly. They experimented with electricity, but the technology was too primitive to be useful at the time. So they turned their efforts to optical means. First they managed to send messages between two points 0.25 miles (0.4 km) apart, using a pendulum attached to a post. In 1791, the Chappes created the first version of an optical semaphore system. It consisted of sending messages between two towers, or stations. On March 2, 1791, they sent the message *"Si vous réussissez, vous serez bientôt couverts de gloire"* ("If you succeed, you will soon be covered with glory") a distance of 9.9 miles (16 km) from Brûlon to Parce.

The system relied on the use of black and white panels, which were observed by telescope from the next station. The colors of the panels used corresponded to a letter. A cipher was used to encode the message, so even if the enemy could tell which letters were being sent, they couldn't read the message.

The brothers took their apparatus to Paris to demonstrate it. But the towers they erected were torn down twice by mobs,

Encoding Telegraphic Messages

A telegraph system cannot transmit words. Instead, it must replace each letter in the word with a number or symbol. Methods of optical signaling have existed since ancient times. An early successful semaphore system was invented by Polybius, a Greek noble held captive in ancient Rome. He accompanied the Roman general Scipio Aemilianus to Carthage during the Third Punic War (149–146 BCE). Observing a need for the army to transmit messages at a distance, he developed a semaphore system. It assigned a pair of numbers to each letter in the alphabet that were transmitted by raised and lowered torches. Methods that replace the letters in a word with numbers are known as ciphers. His method is called the Polybius square.

In the Polybius square, five numbers (say, 1 to 5) are written across the top and five numbers are written down the left side. The letters of the alphabet are arranged from left to right in rows, top to bottom (for the English twenty-six-letter alphabet, two letters, usually *i* and *j*, are combined). The code for each letter is formed by the two numbers that intersect. This method of **encryption** was the most common for centuries after its invention, and many later cipher systems were variations of this approach.

Polybius's code was used to send long-distance messages by means of two groups of torches. The two numbers represented by the torches corresponded to a letter of the alphabet.

Claude Chappe's optical telegraph is shown in this illustration. Inside, the operator can be seen manipulating the apparatus at the top of the tower.

who thought the system was being used by the royalists to send messages for the king. Having spent 40,000 livres of his own money, Claude applied to the Legislative Assembly for police protection for his towers. In May 1792, he was able to arrange a presentation about his system to the assembly. However, the assembly disbanded in September before any action was taken.

In April 1793, Claude Chappe approached the National Convention, which had replaced the Legislative Assembly as the governing body of France. He explained the benefits of using his system. The joint committees on war and public instruction deemed it worthy of a test. The results of the test in July were favorable, and construction started on a series of stations. Claude

Chappe was given the title of "telegraph engineer" and the pay of a lieutenant of engineering in the army. He oversaw the construction of the towers. The first line constructed ran from Paris to Lille.

The telegraph stations looked much like the round stone windmills of the period. They consisted of a tower with a small room for the operator. At the top of the tower was a pole that was 10 feet (3 m) tall or more, with a 14-foot (4.26 m) crossbar called the "regulator" on top. The crossbar was on a pivot. At each end of the crossbar was a 6-foot-long (1.8-meter-long) arm called the "indicator," which could be tilted at any angle by the operator in the control room, by means of wires. The operator could place the regulator and arms into 196 different positions. In practice, 98 positions were used for the content of messages. The regulator and indicators were painted black for maximum visibility. A well-known clockmaker, Abraham-Louis Breguet, designed and built a control mechanism that consisted of a small replica of the semaphore mechanism, connected to the one above the building by means of pulleys, wires, and ropes. The operator moved the parts of the small version, which moved the connections to the large one.

Claude Chappe called on Léon Delaunay, a friend in the diplomatic service, to help devise a code, using his knowledge of the ciphers that sent diplomatic messages. Claude Chappe came up with a code of 9,999 words, later changed to 8,464 words. He compiled these words in a ninety-page codebook. Each page contained ninety-two words and the numbers to encipher them.

To send a message, the agent at one station sent the number of the page as the first signal and the number of the word on the page as the second signal. To speed up the process of sending messages, the Chappes later created a second ninety-two-page codebook that contained common phrases, and a third, which contained place names. From that point on, the operator sent the number of the codebook as the first signal, the page number as the second signal, and the number of the word or phrase as the third signal. Messages could be sent at night by placing lanterns at the ends of the station arms.

A great number of messages were sent from stations while the line was being built. The first message to be sent on the completed line occurred in August 1794 and announced the defeat of the Austrians and the capture of Quesnoy by the French. The message reached Paris only an hour after the French victory.

The benefits of the telegraph were not widely known until September 1, 1794. On that day, the French recaptured the town of Condé, which had been taken by the Austrians. The French minister of war, L. N. M. Carnot, addressed the full National Convention, stating, "Citizens, here is the news just received this instant by the telegraph that you have established from Paris to Lille: 'Condé is restored to the Republic; the retaking took place this morning at six o'clock.'"

The National Convention was enthusiastic and ordered a second line to be built to Landau in Bavaria, as well as an extension of the Lille line to Ostend, Belgium. When the Directoire replaced the

National Convention in 1795, it too saw the benefits of the system, and work continued on it. In 1798, the Lille line was extended to Dunkirk, and two additional lines were added, one from Paris to Brest and one from Paris through Dijon to Lyon. By the end of the revolutionary period in 1800, the system crossed France and represented the first countrywide telecommunications system.

A SYSTEM THAT LASTS

When the republic ended with the ascension of Napoleon to the position of first consul in 1799, Claude Chappe was afraid that financial support for his system would end, and it would fall into disuse. He came up with the idea that the system could be used by businesses for applications such as sending stock quotations, information about ship arrivals, and the like. In particular, the French lottery had been plagued by fraud. Men from Paris had been selling lottery tickets to people in the provinces after the drawing had already taken place but before news of the results arrived. Chappe pointed out that if the results were sent by telegraph immediately, this problem would be eliminated. The Lottery Commission was enthusiastic about the idea and provided Chappe with a large sum of money to implement it.

By 1814, chains of telegraph towers stretched to all frontiers and seaports. Unfortunately, Claude Chappe, suffering from a painful bladder disease and depression, committed suicide in 1805. His brothers, Ignace and Pierre, assumed control of the system, which continued to be used until the mid-nineteenth century, when it was replaced by electrical telegraphy.

Larrey's ambulance service during the Egyptian campaign used camels as a means of transport.

CHAPTER FIVE

The Ambulance

Prior to the French Revolution, wounded soldiers received no treatment during battle. They were collected from the battlefield once the battle was over, which could be a day or more after they were wounded. From the 1500s until the mid-1700s, when the survivors were removed, stretchers called litters were used to carry them from the field to the rear of the line, where they received medical care from servants, **camp followers**, and local people, none of whom had any medical training. The French Revolution did not just see improvements in weapons. Improvements in transporting and treating wounded soldiers also occurred, including the ambulance and battlefield medical teams.

THE HISTORY OF BATTLEFIELD MEDICINE

The concept of organized medical care for soldiers did exist in ancient times. During the Roman Empire, the Romans, who maintained a very large professional army, made formal arrangements for the treatment of wounded soldiers—both their own and captured enemy soldiers. They maintained a regular army medical corps with physicians who treated soldiers both on the battlefield and in facilities in Roman forts. Soldiers with various levels of medical training were part of each Roman legion. These legionnaires were primarily soldiers, but they also provided medical care. The significant time and cost it took to train skilled Roman legionnaires meant that keeping them healthy and able to fight was worth the investment in medical personnel. In addition, captured soldiers and civilians were valuable as slaves, who were used for skilled and unskilled labor. Because they were an important part of the Roman economy, the Romans preferred to take prisoners rather than kill those they conquered, as was common in the wars of later eras.

In the Middle Ages, some surgeons and doctors did accompany armies, but they mostly treated officers. As mentioned, wounded soldiers were not collected until after the battle was over. In some cases, they were placed in the care of local citizens, and in some situations, the locals then demanded ransom for the return of the soldiers.

When many European countries began maintaining large standing armies in the 1400s, barber-surgeons were often paid to accompany the forces and treat the wounded after the battle was over, as well as tend to those who could not move on with the army. Carts either provided by the army or commandeered from locals were used to transport soldiers to the rear of the line after battle, for treatment.

In the seventeenth century, for the first time, field and military hospitals and homes for disabled soldiers were established. The first permanent military hospital, the Hôtel des Invalides, was established by King Louis XIV in Paris in 1674, and the first English military hospital was opened in 1684. In the early eighteenth century, Louis XIV ordered the construction of fifty-one military hospitals staffed by two hundred surgeons and doctors. By the middle of the seventeenth century, military medical units set up field hospitals behind the lines, where they performed surgery and treatment. However, this still took place after the battle, at the rear of the line.

DOMINIQUE-JEAN LARREY

Like others, doctors and medical students found themselves drawn into the revolution. One such doctor was Dominique-Jean Larrey (1766–1842). Larrey was born in a small village in the Pyrenees Mountains. When he was orphaned at the age of thirteen, he moved in with an uncle in Toulouse, France. His uncle was the chief surgeon in Toulouse, and Larrey became a medical apprentice. After six years as an apprentice, he went to Paris to continue his medical studies. In 1786, Larrey joined the navy and traveled to North America. Not long after, however, he

Dominique-Jean Larrey

quit the navy due to chronic seasickness and returned to Paris to complete his thesis.

Surgeons were typically from the middle or working class and trained by apprenticeship. Most opposed the monarchy and the privileged classes and institutions. On the day the Bastille was stormed, July 14, 1789, Larrey led a contingent of fifteen hundred medical students to the site. They armed themselves at the Hôtel des Invalides then marched to the Bastille, attracting the people to the revolution along the way. Throughout his life, Larrey was a strong believer in the ideals of the revolution.

THE AMBULANCE

When war broke out in 1792, Larrey joined the French Army of the Rhine as medical chief of a division. He took part in more than sixty battles. Among the innovations he introduced to military medicine were a curved needle for stitching wounds and the use of **camphorated** wine, or Labarraque's solution, to wash wounds, thereby reducing infections. However, his greatest contribution was the introduction of improved techniques for evacuating wounded soldiers from the battlefield and treating them on the spot.

Warfare in the era of the French Revolution was producing greater numbers of wounded soldiers than in past eras. This increase was in part due to widespread conscription—the vast numbers of men being drafted into the army and the use of multiple large formations of troops naturally meant greater numbers of wounded. It was also the result of the innovations in weaponry. Improvements in muskets had made them more accurate and therefore more deadly, but the really devastating weapon was the new mobile artillery of the 1790s, which could easily be moved into position to attack these vast formations. The large mass of projectiles from a group of artillery pieces all hitting at once resulted in shattering wounds that often required the amputation of a limb. The traditional method for performing an amputation was to wait several days before carrying out the operation. This approach usually resulted in infected wounds and a high rate of death among patients. Larrey believed that performing the surgery sooner would reduce the number of people who died.

At the time Larrey became medical chief, surgeons treated wounded soldiers at the rear of the army. They worked on *fourgons* (long covered wagons used for carrying baggage and supplies), drawn by at least forty horses. Most of the wounded soldiers walked or were carried by comrades to the rear of the army. Because the vehicles were so cumbersome, they typically did not reach the actual point of battle until about thirty-six hours after the battle. By that time, most of the soldiers who were too badly wounded to reach the rear of the line were dead. To combat this problem, Larrey came up with the idea of creating *ambulances volante* ("flying ambulances"), a form of light transportation that could follow the advance guard of the army onto the field in the same manner as the new light artillery. These "flying ambulance" teams would provide emergency medical care on the field and transport the wounded away from the battle.

The traditional method of battle, in which rows of soldiers stood shoulder to shoulder in tight formation, firing at the enemy a couple of hundred yards away, would have made his idea impossible. However, Napoleon had revolutionized battlefield tactics, using smaller, more mobile units arranged in more open formations around a very large field of battle. This provided room for Larrey's flying ambulances.

Larrey secured a number of two- and four-wheeled light wagons. He staffed them with medical officers and their assistants, and they moved with the front line during battle. The ambulances moved around the field of battle, treating fallen soldiers and those who walked to the wagons. The surgeons performed amputations and dressed wounds on site and then transported the treated soldiers back to the field hospital. Larrey also established a system of triage—treating patients according to the severity of their wounds. He decreed that those who were most seriously wounded were to be treated first, without regard to rank or distinction, whereas those less seriously injured would be treated afterward. This was a radical departure from the traditional approach, whereby officers and nobles were treated first, regardless of the seriousness of their wounds, while ordinary soldiers had to wait.

FLYING AMBULANCE UNITS

Larrey continued to work on improving his flying ambulance units. They reached their final form in 1796. He created ambulance units that were composed of 340 men divided into three divisions, and assigned one unit for every ten thousand soldiers. Each unit had eight two-wheeled wagons drawn by horses, for use in flat terrain, and four four-wheeled wagons drawn by four horses, for hilly land.

Pierre-François Percy

Another surgeon who improved battlefield medical treatment and the transportation of patients was Pierre-François Percy (1754–1825). Percy was the son of a French village surgeon. Following in his father's footsteps, he studied to become a surgeon. When the government created the medical service in 1776, Percy joined it, and in 1782 he became a surgeon in the Cavalry Regiment of Berri. Throughout the revolution, he served in the army at various locations.

He designed a mobile hospital modeled on the light infantry wagons. It took its name from the Austrian Wurtz wagon works and was called "the Wurtz." Each hospital wagon was pulled by six horses. It was staffed by eight surgeons and 120 orderlies. It contained enough instruments, stretchers, and supplies to treat 1,200 soldiers. Although it was mobile enough to accompany the army, it was too large to move around the battlefield. Therefore, it was placed near the line in a safe spot, and soldiers walked or were brought to it for treatment. Percy's mobile hospital wagon provided a treatment station for soldiers who otherwise would have had to walk or be carried to the hospital train located several miles away.

Larrey had the wagons specially outfitted to carry the wounded. Each wagon consisted of an oblong box suspended on springs to help minimize the jarring of injured soldiers. The wagons had a door at both the front and rear, and shutters on the sides. The two-wheeled wagons each carried two injured soldiers, and the four-wheeled wagons each carried four. Four storage wagons and one hundred support staff, including fourteen surgeons, completed each unit.

A major advantage of Larrey's system was that it allowed soldiers who needed amputations to have the operation done quickly, while they were still in shock and the limb was numb. In the days before anesthetics, this was a great benefit and also increased the patient's chance of survival. Seventy percent of patients requiring this surgery survived if it was done immediately, whereas only 10 percent survived if they had to wait a week. Larrey's flying ambulances revolutionized the way the wounded were handled.

Napoleon leads the French troops at the Battle of Marengo in Italy.

CHAPTER SIX

The Aftermath of the Revolution

Napoleon's military ambitions did not end when the revolution did. From 1800 to 1815 he continued to lead France in a series of wars against various coalitions of European countries. These conflicts are referred to collectively as the Napoleonic Wars. In addition to defeating two coalitions during the French Revolutionary Wars, Napoleon was victorious over three more during the Napoleonic Wars before losing to the sixth and seventh coalitions in 1814 and 1815.

ARTILLERY IN THE NAPOLEONIC WARS

Throughout his career, Napoleon continued to use artillery to his advantage, and the number and power of artillery pieces continued to increase. For example, the French Army of Italy had sixty artillery pieces. During the Napoleonic Wars at the Battle of Borodino in 1812, the total artillery employed by both sides equaled 1,200 pieces, which fired about 15,000 rounds per hour along a 2-mile (3.2 km) battlefront.

One of the aspects that made Napoleon so successful was his use of artillery. Most armies of the time relied on artillery to protect the infantry and cavalry. Napoleon instead used artillery as an offensive weapon. He deployed it first to destroy and disrupt the opposing army, allowing the infantry and cavalry to strike the final blow that would win the battle. For instance, at the Battle of Austerlitz in 1805, there were 2 artillery pieces for every one thousand men. By 1809, at the Battle of Wagram, there were 4 artillery pieces per one thousand men, and at the Battle of Borodino in 1812, there were 4.5 artillery pieces per one thousand men.

Napoleon continued to look for ways to improve French artillery. He was quick to see the advantages of the British shrapnells, a type of cast-iron shell loaded with musket balls, held in place by resin or melted sulfur, and gunpowder. The shrapnells went farther and scattered their contents a longer distance than older shells. When the French captured a howitzer and two wagons of British shrapnells at the Battle of Albuera in 1811, Napoleon ordered experiments to be carried out to determine how to use them.

Under the Gribeauval system, many of the parts of artillery guns were interchangeable. However, there were still twenty-five different sizes of wheels. Also, each caliber of gun rested on a unique carriage. Napoleon wanted a more efficient system. In 1803, the System of Year XI replaced the Gribeauval system. One advance with the new system was that the cannon and carriage were lighter than in Gribeauval's system, which made them even more maneuverable.

Eventually, the advances in artillery moved it to the forefront of the modern battlefield. By the time of the Battle of Friedland in 1807 during the Napoleonic Wars, artillery had become a military unit of equal importance with the infantry and cavalry. At Friedland, General Alexandre-Antoine Hureau de Sénarmont (1769–1810), chief of the French First Artillery Corps, took the initiative to carry out an artillery attack against the center of the Russian forces.

Friedland, then a part of Prussia (now Pravdinsk in Russia), sits on a loop of the Alle River. The general in charge of the Russian army in the battle, Levin August Bennigsen (1745–1826), found that a corps of the French army led by Marshal Jean Lannes occupied the west bank of the river without any other forces in the area. Bennigsen had his forces build three bridges across the river, in addition to using an existing bridge, to cross it and attack Lannes's troops before the main army could reach them. Lannes had twenty-six thousand troops, whereas Bennigsen had sixty thousand. Lannes sent messengers to alert Napoleon of their plight. When Napoleon arrived with troops that evening, he found the French had held off Bennigsen's army. He initiated an attack on the Russians, but his troops were stopped by a massive artillery attack from the Russian battery and driven back.

At the center of the French forces, General Pierre Dupont (1765–1840) commanded an infantry division. He advanced, supported by twelve artillery guns. At that point, Sénarmont, in charge of the artillery corps, requested that the entire artillery, consisting of thirty-six guns, be allowed to advance with Dupont. Gaining permission, Sénarmont divided the artillery into two fifteen-gun batteries, reserving the other six guns. He placed one battery on each side of Dupont's division. The artillery batteries moved faster than the main body of the troops and soon found themselves ahead of Dupont's other forces. Sénarmont took the initiative and ordered the artillery forward, opening fire at the center of the Russian forces when they were 450 yards (410 m) away. They fired half a dozen salvos, then Sénarmont ordered them to close to within 250 yards (230 m). The artillery opened fire again. Sénarmont repeated this maneuver at a distance of 100 to 150 yards (90–135 m) and ordered the artillery to loose a rapid-fire barrage. In a mere twenty minutes, the Russian center was destroyed. Dupont closed in with the infantry and defeated the remaining Russian infantry. The Russian cavalry tried to attack Sénarmont, but two volleys from the artillery ended their charge. As the Russians ran for the bridges, Dupont and Sénarmont's forces advanced on Friedland, destroying most of the remaining Russian army. Afterward, Sénarmont started a school of artillery tactics, and his use of artillery was employed in other battles.

SAVING SOLDIERS' LIVES

Dominique-Jean Larrey and Pierre-François Percy continued to implement advances in battlefield medicine during the Napoleonic Wars. During the Spanish campaign under General Jean-Victor-Marie Moreau (1763–1813), Percy addressed the problem of how to get soldiers off the battlefield without waiting for the end of the battle. He organized and trained a stretcher-bearer corps, called *brancardiers* ("litter bearers"). They worked in pairs, each equipped with a lance and a sash. When necessary, the two sashes were tied between the two lances, a wounded soldier was laid on the resulting stretcher, and he was carried off the field to the medical station at the rear of the line of battle. Each hospital unit was assigned thirty-two brancardiers.

The French army officially recognized the brancardier system in the Decree of 1813, and it became the foundation for the later regimental bearer corps in the French army. Percy also advocated for medical personnel, medical stores, and hospital stations to be considered "neutral" participants on the battlefield, meaning they should not be targets of the enemy. This concept was incorporated into the Geneva Convention of 1864, which was signed by all major countries and covers the rules by which warfare is to be conducted. The systems introduced by Percy and Larrey influenced other European armies. By the middle of the nineteenth century, most European armies included some form of ambulance wagons and stretcher bearers.

The French system of flying ambulances and medical care eventually carried over to America in the nineteenth century. As late as the Mexican-American War (1846–1848), America had no organized system of medical treatment or transportation for wounded soldiers. From 1854 to 1856, the Crimean War took place in Europe. A coalition of European countries, including France, fought against the Russians over control of the Crimean Peninsula on the Black Sea. In the United Sates at the time, Jefferson Davis was secretary of war. He sent a military commission to the scene of the war around Sevastopol to observe any new methods of warfare. He instructed them to study "the kind of ambulances and other means of transporting the sick and wounded." The members of the commission observed the ambulance systems used by the French as well as other European countries. Upon their return, they reported to Congress, explaining the method of ambulance transport and the methods of moving wounded soldiers from the field using methods such as handheld litters and litters carried like pack saddles on mules. They also covered hospital carts and their staffs and the organization by which soldiers were transported from the field to a field hospital and then to permanent hospitals. The methods they described would eventually form the basis of a new system of medical transportation during the Civil War.

Ambulance wagons were not used in US armies prior to the Civil War. During the War of 1812, surgeon James Mann wrote a report in which he suggested the use of a system of hospital

This type of horse-drawn ambulance was used during the American Civil War. The American ambulance service took many of its elements from the French system.

wagons and the flying ambulances as used in Larrey's system, but the system was not implemented. The first US ambulance wagon was designed in 1858. However, at the outbreak of the Civil War neither the Union nor Confederate army had an organized system for transporting the wounded. It was not until 1862 that a divisional army medical corps was established with ambulance wagons. When it was formed, it was closely modeled on Larrey's system with two- and four-wheeled ambulance wagons and a triage system whereby soldiers were treated near the battle, then sent to a field hospital, and ultimately moved to a permanent hospital. The final system combined elements of Larrey's flying ambulances and Percy's stretcher bearers.

Prussian Flying Medical Units

An example of the adoption of battlefield emergency medical treatment is provided by the Prussian army of the mid-1800s. The Prussian army provided a light hospital to each division. Attached to each light hospital was a "bearer company," consisting of 202 staff members with 45 stretchers. The flying medical detachment dressed wounds, applied tourniquets to stop bleeding, and performed operations vital to keeping wounded soldiers alive. Those less critically injured could go directly to a medical station located in a safe spot near the battlefield or a hospital facility away from the battlefield. The medical station was manned by five doctors, a pharmacist, and ten assistants. It had a medicine wagon, a bandage wagon, and four ambulance wagons for transporting the seriously wounded. Behind the lines, usually at a farm or a village, was an area staffed by medical personnel who oversaw the transportation of the wounded to a permanent hospital facility. This type of system, which stemmed directly from the French approach, remained the basis for battlefield medical treatment all the way to World War I.

Emergency treatment by flying medical units reduced the number of soldiers who died on the battlefield or from infections that resulted from delayed treatment. In addition, it kept soldiers from using the fact that they needed to assist an injured soldier to the field hospital as an excuse to leave the field of battle. It also resolved the problem of injured soldiers becoming the victims of thieves as they lay for long periods on the field.

TELEGRAPHY IN THE NINETEENTH CENTURY

When Napoleon seized power in 1799, he ordered the telegraph system created by the Chappe brothers to be extended. Included in the new lines he requested was one that extended across the English Channel because, at the time, he planned an invasion of Britain, although this never came to pass. New lines continued to be added to the telegraph system until 1846, although some lines in foreign areas no longer occupied by the French were dismantled. The network formed essentially a star pattern with Paris at the center and lines extending outward in all directions.

The government of France was constantly in flux during the nineteenth century, alternating between empires, monarchies, and republican governments. From 1830 to 1848, the country was ruled by King Louis-Philippe (1773–1850). During his reign, France engaged in significant colonization. Among the countries ruled by France at the time were Algeria and Morocco, and three lines were added to the Chappe telegraph system to allow communication within those colonies.

The Chappe telegraph system continued to be used for sixty-one years. The last message received by the system was the French victory at Sebastopol, a port on the Black Sea in the Crimean Peninsula, during the Crimean War (October 1853–March 1856). After that, it was replaced by electrical telegraph systems.

The success of the optical telegraph fueled people's desire to be able to communicate at a distance. People wanted news, businesses wanted to exchange information with customers,

This drawing shows one of Claude Chappe's telegraph towers in Algeria.

investors wanted information on the stock market, and as always, governments wanted to be able to quickly communicate news and instructions to troops in the field. As far back as the early eighteenth century there had been interest in using electricity to send telegraphic messages. However, the lack of adequate material blocked researchers' efforts. In the nineteenth century, progress was finally made. In Europe, Pavel Schilling (1786–1837), a Russian diplomat serving in Germany, created the first electrical telegraph in 1832. Other European inventors soon succeeded in making working electrical telegraphs as well. American inventors interested in making long-distance communication possible in the United States began working on an electrical version of the telegraph, too.

Samuel F. B. Morse completed a working version of the electrical recording telegraph in 1837. Soon telegraph lines crossed countries everywhere. Intercontinental telegraph lines were built, too. The last country to be connected by telegraph was Australia in 1872. With the completion of Australia's system, it became possible to send information telegraphically worldwide. The railway industry was one of the major users of the telegraph, which made it possible to transmit information about when trains would depart and arrive. As with the optical telegraph, the military used the electrical telegraph to transmit orders and receive information. For example, during the American Civil War, both the Union and the Confederacy relied on telegraphy.

In France, the first electrical telegraph was installed in 1846. This version of the telegraph continued to transmit messages by using electricity to operate a Chappe-style optical system. It was replaced in 1855 with a Morse-style telegraph system.

Despite the fact that it had limitations, such as not being able to operate in adverse weather conditions that limited visibility, the optical telegraph system provided the model for the electrical telegraph systems of the mid-1800s. It demonstrated the method by which messages could be encoded and sent over a network for great distances rapidly and paved the way for modern communications systems.

Modern mobile artillery includes a variety of guns and types of shells. It is armored to protect the crew that drives and fires it.

CHAPTER SEVEN

Lasting Effects

The eighteenth century in many ways was the beginning of the modern scientific era. The activities of scientists and engineers laid the foundation for the inventions not only of the nineteenth century but also of the twentieth and twenty-first centuries.

NAPOLEONIC ARTILLERY AND MODERN WARFARE

Many of the tactics used by Napoleon are still studied and applied in modern warfare. Mobile artillery has continued to be a key part of warfare in the past two centuries. Artillery reigned supreme in World War I as it had in the French Revolutionary Wars.

Even with military aircraft and naval vessels, wars are still primarily won and lost by infantry—commonly called "boots on the ground." The number-one weapon against infantry troops—and tanks, which had become part of the military arsenal by World War I—is artillery. Howitzers and mortars continued to be used. Artillery in the twentieth century was still divided into light, medium, and heavy guns. Shrapnel-filled shells continued to be used as well.

The most popular artillery gun in World War I was the French 75mm Model 1897 field gun. Its design improved on earlier artillery models by incorporating a recoil mechanism that allowed gunners to fire several shots without having to reload the gun. However, the fact that soldiers in World War I dug trenches and fought from them made it necessary to modify artillery again so that it would be effective for trench warfare.

Napoleon's employment of mobile artillery continues to be a mainstay of modern warfare. However, today the military has self-propelled artillery that is motorized so that it can move to a target without being towed. The motorized howitzer is an example of self-propelled artillery. Some types of motorized artillery resemble tanks because they consist of a gun placed on a base that moves on continuous tracks. The gun can be a large howitzer, a mortar, or a rocket or missile launcher. Large guns are often used for long-range bombardment of the enemy.

Self-propelled artillery was first used during World War I. During World War II, artillery included heavily armored self-propelled assault guns and tank destroyers. Assault guns accompanied infantry and provided close-fire support; tank destroyers are special-use antitank vehicles. Although self-propelled artillery was used during World Wars I and II, towed artillery continued to be used as well. It was pulled by tractors or by draft horses. Today, most artillery is self propelled.

As in Napoleon's day, the key to the effective use of artillery is bringing it into action as quickly as possible. Speed of deployment is the major advantage of self-propelled artillery. It can move into action much more quickly than towed artillery. Also, towed artillery could not just be put into place and used immediately. Once in position, the gun had to be unfastened, unpacked, and set up. When the time came to move it to a new position, the gun had to be secured again and towed to a new location. Self-propelled artillery does not need to be set up. It can drive to the desired location and be used right away, then quickly move on to a new location. This is a valuable feature when a force is advancing.

Towed artillery does have some uses in modern-day warfare. It is lighter and smaller than self-propelled artillery, and therefore can be used in places where self-propelled artillery cannot fit. It can be carried by transport helicopters for rapid deployment, and it is cheaper to build and maintain. So towed artillery is still part of the arsenal of many armies.

FROM TELEGRAPH TO CELL PHONE

The telegraph gave rise to new forms of communication systems. Although the telegraph systems developed by Claude Chappe and Samuel F. B. Morse are no longer in use today, their direct descendants are. It is easy to see the telegraphic ancestry of modern communication systems. The optical and wired telegraph systems gave rise to "wireless radiotelegraphy," or "radio" and "wireless technology," as it is known today.

The invention of radio (wireless telegraphy) was an international effort. During the late 1880s, German scientist Heinrich Hertz (1857–1894) proved that electricity can be transmitted in **electromagnetic** waves. He experimented with sending and receiving these waves. Nikola Tesla (1856–1943), a Serbian American inventor, discovered how to wirelessly transmit electromagnetic energy. In 1893, he performed the first public demonstration of radio in St. Louis. An Italian electrical engineer, Guglielmo Marconi (1874–1937), independently developed a wireless radiotelegraphy apparatus. He filed for a patent and in 1897 formed the Wireless Telegraph and Signal Company in the United Kingdom.

By 1891, radios began to appear on ships. This technology is called "wireless telegraphy" today. It allowed the transmission of coded messages in much the same way as land-based telegraph systems, but without wires. Shipboard radios improved the safety of ships by allowing them to receive weather and other types of information while at sea. In 1899, the *R. F. Matthews* became the first ship to request emergency assistance using a shipboard radio (Marconi's system).

Guglielmo Marconi, Italian radio pioneer and physicist, demonstrates one of his early radios.

Marconi continued to make advances in long-distance telegraphy. In 1901, he sent the first transatlantic signal, from Ireland to Canada. His technology made it possible for the first time for people around the world to talk to each other via wireless technology. One year later, *Scientific American* magazine published an article, "How to Construct an Efficient Wireless Telegraphy Apparatus at Small Cost." Amateur radio fans started building such systems and using them to communicate, an activity that became a popular hobby called "ham" radio. Reginald Fessenden (1866–1932) was a Canadian inventor who established a way of transmitting continuous radio waves rather than individual electrical pulses. The use of continuous waves made it possible to transmit voice and music via radio in addition to telegraphic messages. In 1900, Fessenden went to work for the US Weather Bureau with the goal of replacing the existing telegraphic system with radio transmissions from coastal radio stations. He was the first to succeed in transmitting a voice message via radio. In 1906, he was the first person to use radio to transmit a program of speech and music.

In 1906, Lee de Forest (1873–1961), an American scientist who played a key role in radio and the development of sound for motion pictures, created the Audion, a triode vacuum tube that allowed for amplification of radio signals. The amplification allowed the signals to be transmitted over much longer distances. In 1918, the first radio transmission from an airplane took place. In World War I and World War II, radio became the major means by which military information was transmitted, replacing the telegraphic systems used in earlier wars.

In the early 1920s, researchers, including those at the Marconi Company and Bell Laboratories, evolved concepts for cellular radio telephony. The necessary technology was understood by 1945. In that year, a *Saturday Evening Post* article appeared, titled "Phone Me by Air." It quoted Federal Communications Commissioner E. K. Jett saying that zones could be established in which different frequencies could be used for different channels, half of which could be used at the same time without overlapping. Bell Laboratories produced the first commercial mobile radio telephone system in America in 1946, although it was not yet a cellular system. Companies around the world developed cellular phone systems throughout the 1950s and 1960s. Motorola's Martin Cooper is credited with the invention of the first personal, handheld cellular radio telephone, in 1973.

THE INTERNET AND COMMUNICATION

The internet is a network of computers connected by wired and wireless technology around the world. Its development was initially funded by the Defense Advanced Research Projects Agency (DARPA) of the US Defense Department, starting in the 1960s. The goal was to create a broadly distributed communications network that would allow military communications to continue if the existing land-based communication system was knocked out by a war. In the 1980s, DARPA made the internet available for commercial and business use. During this period, British computer scientist Tim Berners-Lee developed a computer language, hypertext markup language (HTML), that allowed anyone to create webpages with embedded links (hyperlinks) to other pages, creating the World Wide Web. The combination of wireless radio technology with the internet has changed both military and civilian communication and created a system that allows communication and commerce to be conducted between people anywhere in the world.

EMERGENCY MEDICINE

Dominique-Jean Larrey is considered by many to be the father of emergency medicine. His system of triage is still used as the basis for treating patients in disasters, on battlefields, and in emergency rooms. His flying ambulances and battlefield medical units set the **precedent** for field ambulances and medical corps in wars all the way to the present. They were also the ancestors of modern ambulances used in civilian emergency medical care.

The Civil War brought knowledge of ambulances and emergency medicine, based on Larrey's system, to civilian authorities. The first civilian ambulance was put to use in Cincinnati, Ohio, at Commercial Hospital, just after the Civil War ended in 1865. In 1869, Edward Dalton, a former Union army surgeon, was commissioned to create an ambulance service for Bellevue Hospital in New York City to bring patients to the hospital more rapidly. These ambulances were horse-drawn and equipped with first-aid supplies used at the time, such as splints and bandages, a stomach pump, brandy, and morphine for pain.

Initially, Dalton ordered that the horses pulling the ambulances be harnessed at all times to ensure that the ambulance could respond immediately to an emergency. In a matter of months, a

Chappe and the Internet Connection

Interestingly, Chappe's optical telegraph network in the nineteenth century has many similarities with the internet of today. It allowed for messages to be transmitted, even internationally, at a speed previously unheard of in its day. It was developed initially by the military for military communications and later opened up to commercial enterprises. Similarly, the creation of the internet was funded by the US Defense Department. Its original purpose was to ensure the ability of the government to communicate in the event of war. Later, it was made available for commercial use by businesses. On the negative side, like the internet, the Chappe system could be used for fraud and scams.

Although Chappe's optical telegraph system was composed of mechanical parts that may seem primitive compared to today's electronic systems, it used many of the same processes employed by computer-based communications systems like the internet today. Among these processes are **control signals**, **synchronization**, and **flow control protocols**. Like the internet, the Chappe system was a game-changing technology, reducing the time needed to send messages from days to hours or less. However, because of a French law prohibiting the setting up of private telegraph networks, it never had the impact on the lives of the general public that the internet does.

One of Dr. Dalton's horse-drawn ambulances, circa 1896. A doctor with an instrument case accompanies the ambulance to provide emergency treatment to the patient.

"drop harness" arrangement was created. It consisted of a harness setup that was lowered from the ceiling, by means of a pulley, right onto the horses, so that they could be outfitted within thirty seconds. Thus, the horses did not need to be in harness continuously, and no time was lost in reaching the patient. The success of the ambulances was easy to see. In 1870, they responded to 1,401 emergencies; in 1891, they responded to 4,392 calls. For the first week of their operation, the ambulances were crewed by the hospital's house staff, after which the hospital hired Drs. Duncan Lee and Robert Taylor as full-time ambulance surgeons. Going forward, the plan was to use recent graduates of the hospital's surgical training program to crew the ambulances. Dalton planned to rotate the graduates so that they would be replaced by the next batch of graduates each time a new class graduated. However, the graduates objected to both the schedule of twelve-hour shifts and the low salary offered. By the end of 1869, Dalton instead was assigning residents-in-training to staff the ambulances, since they had no choice but to do whatever they were assigned to do.

The invention of the automobile profoundly changed transportation, including that used for medical treatment. By the first years of the twentieth century, militaries around the world were experimenting with motorized ambulances, which ran on electricity, steam, or gasoline. The first motorized ambulance was put into service at Michael Reese Hospital in Chicago in 1899. The first wide-scale use of motorized ambulances occurred in World War I.

In the 1960s, ambulances changed from being merely transportation to the hospital to being emergency medical service vehicles. Studies showed the high number of people killed and injured in highway accidents, and the need for on-site prehospital treatment for the victims of auto accidents. In 1966, the National Highway and Traffic Administration established standards for ambulances. In the same period, qualifications and training for

A patient is loaded into an early motorized ambulance. Motorization significantly decreased the time it took to transport patients to the hospital.

the first emergency medical technicians (EMTs) to crew the ambulances were laid out. This standardization of vehicle and crew resulted in the first nationally recognized curriculum for ambulance-based EMTs in 1969. The emphasis on emergency treatment led to the creation of emergency medical service and the specialty of emergency medicine. At the same time, the first paramedics were created during the Vietnam War.

Modern ambulances are built on truck and van chassis. They incorporate features such as custom tail lifts, ramps, winches, cabinetry for medical supplies, special lighting, and computer and radio communication equipment. They have a large cabin space and the equipment to perform a variety of medical services while in transit. EMTs can start intravenous fluids, monitor vital signs like heart rate and blood pressure, dress wounds, and even attempt to restart a patient's heart while on the move. They can give medications under the direction of a physician.

Even though ambulances today look nothing like the horse-drawn wagons of the 1790s, their function is the same: to stabilize patients and get them to the hospital in a swift fashion.

The fighting between the French and various other European countries did not end with the demise of the French Republic. After a brief period of peace, lasting only until 1803, refusals by both France and Britain to give up territories they thought in their best interest to keep led to a new round of wars—the Napoleonic Wars between France and various coalitions of Britain and other European countries. Napoleon continued to make use of the technology that had served him so well in the French Revolutionary Wars.

GLOSSARY

anticlerical Against the activities of clergy in public affairs.

arbitrary Having no justification other than one's will.

camp follower A civilian who accompanies an army and provides a service.

camphorated Made of camphor, a chemical compound used to treat pain, itching, and infection.

coalition A temporary alliance.

combustion The process by which oxygen is used to burn a material.

conscription Drafting people into an army.

constitutional monarchy A form of limited monarchy, which usually includes a monarch and an organized group of representatives of the people.

control signal A signal sent from the sender to the receiver to indicate a message is being sent.

depleted Used up.

depose To remove from a position of power or authority.

deprivation The state in which people lack the necessities of life.

disperse To scatter or spread widely.

electromagnetic Having electric and magnetic properties.

encryption The act of concealing a message through numbers, letters, or symbols.

faction A subgroup within a political party.

flow control protocols Rules for managing the physical transmission of information so it neither gets backed up nor overwhelms the receiving system.

homogeneous The same throughout.

inalienable Not able to be separated or taken away.

inherent Existing permanently and inseparably in a person or thing.

partisan A supporter of a cause.

precedent An act or decision that serves as a guideline for future similar situations.

semaphore A form of signaling in which a physical object, such as a flag or torch, is used to represent numbers or letters.

shrapnel Metal shot or small sharp pieces of material that do damage on impact.

synchronization Making sure elements required for communication are the same at both ends.

tenet A belief.

BIBLIOGRAPHY

Alder, Ken. *Engineering the Revolution: Arms & Enlightenment in France, 1763–1815*. Chicago, IL: University of Chicago Press, 2010.

Andrews, Evan. "Eight Things You May Not Know About the Guillotine." History.com, September 15, 2014. http://www.history.com/news/history-lists/8-things-you-may-not-know-about-the-guillotine.

Bruce, Robert B., Iain Dickie, Kevin Khey, Michael F. Pavkovic, and Frederick C. Schneid. *Fighting Techniques of the Napoleonic Age: 1792–1815: Equipment, Combat Skills, and Tactics*. New York: St. Martin's Press, 2008.

Burbeck, James. "Napoleonic Artillery: Firepower Comes of Age." *War Times Journal*. Retrieved May 9, 2016. http://www.wtj.com/articles/napart.

Chemical Heritage Foundation. "Antoine-Laurent Lavoisier." Retrieved May 9, 2016. http://www.chemheritage.org/discover/online-resources/chemistry-in-history/themes/early-chemistry-and-gases/lavoisier.aspx.

Dihac, J-M. "The Telegraph of Claude Chappe – An Optical Telecommunication Network for the XVIIIth Century." Retrieved April 16, 2016. http://www.ieeeghn.org/wiki/images/1/17/Dilhac.pdf.

Encyclopedia Britannica. "French Revolutionary Wars." Retrieved April 20, 2016. http://www.britannica.com/event/French-revolutionary-wars.

——. "Guillotine." Retrieved April 19, 2016. http://www.britannica.com/topic/guillotine.

Federal Communications Commission. "A Short History of Radio." Retrieved May 12, 2016. https://transition.fcc.gov/omd/history/radio/documents/short_history.pdf.

Gratzer, Walter. *Terrors of the Table: The Curious History of Nutrition*. New York: Oxford University Press, 2005.

Haller, John S., Jr. *Battlefield Medicine: A History of the Military Ambulance from the Napoleonic Wars through World War I.* Carbondale, IL: Southern Illinois University Press, 2011.

History.com Staff. "French Revolution." History.com. Retrieved April 13, 2016. http://www.history.com/topics/french-revolution.

Leiner, Barry M., et al. "A Brief History of the Internet." Internet Society. Retrieved May 12, 2016. http://www.internetsociety.org/internet/what-internet/history-internet/brief-history-internet.

McCallum, Jack E. *Military Medicine from Ancient Times to the 21st Century*. Santa Barbara, CA: ABC-CLIO, 2008.

Pincock, Stephen. *Codebreaker: The History of Codes and Ciphers, from the Ancient Pharaohs to Quantum Cryptography*. New York: Walker, 2006.

Schofield, Hugh. "How Napoleon's Semaphore Telegraph Changed the World." BBC News, June 17, 2013. http://www.bbc.com/news/magazine-22909590.

ShoreTel. "History of the Telegraph in Communications." Retrieved May 10, 2016. https://www.shoretel.com/history-telegraph-communications.

———. "The History of Telecommunications." Retrieved May 12, 2016. https://www.shoretel.com/history-telecommunication.

Weekly Driver News Service. "History of Ambulance Vehicles." *Weekly Driver*, March 14, 2014. https://theweeklydriver.com/history-ambulance-vehicles.

FURTHER INFORMATION

Websites

European History Online (EGO): The French Revolutionary and Napoleonic Wars

http://ieg-ego.eu/en/threads/alliances-and-wars/war-as-an-agent-of-transfer/frederick-c-schneid-the-french-revolutionary-and-napoleonic-wars

EGO provides a detailed description of the French Revolutionary Wars.

EyeWitness to History: The Beginning of the French Revolution, 1789

http://www.eyewitnesstohistory.com/frenchrevolution.htm

A first-person description of the start of the French Revolution is given by Thomas Jefferson, who was minister to France for the United States at the time.

History World: The French Revolutionary Wars

http://www.historyworld.net/wrldhis/PlainTextHistories.asp?ParagraphID=MDI

This website offers historical information, timelines, a quiz, and more.

Liberty, Equality, Fraternity

http://chnm.gmu.edu/revolution

This website contains articles, images, and documents related to the French Revolution.

Videos

Empires: Napoleon

This PBS Home Video production describes Napoleon's rise, accomplishments, campaigns, and exile.

The French Revolution

A History Channel documentary on DVD that describes this period with reenactments, illustrations, accounts from journals, and commentary from historians.

Living the French Revolution and the Age of Napoleon

A twenty-five-part series by the Teaching Company covering various events, people, and military campaigns. (Available as individual episodes from Amazon.com as well as on DVD).

Napoleon

This A&E Biography covers Napoleon's background and military exploits.

The Scarlet Pimpernel

A movie based on Baroness Orczy's novel of the French Revolution.

A Tale of Two Cities

The movie version of Charles Dickens's classic tale.

INDEX

Page numbers in **boldface** are illustrations. Entries in **boldface** are glossary terms.

ABOUT THE AUTHOR

Jeri Freedman has a bachelor of arts from Harvard University. She worked for a number of years in the education department of the Anti-Defamation League in programs providing information on the Holocaust to history teachers. She then worked for fifteen years at high-technology companies. She is the author of more than fifty young adult nonfiction books, including *Tech in the Trenches: Strategic Inventions of World War II*, *A Documentary History of the Holocaust: The Warsaw Ghetto and Uprising*, and *Special Ops: Airborne Commandos*.